The Burley Tobacco Growers Cooperative Association is proud to sponsor *Barns of Kentucky* for the benefit of Kentucky's FFA Youth Program.

BARNS *of* KENTUCKY

compiled by the
kentucky vocational
agriculture teacher's
association

This book is dedicated to all the agriculture teachers/FFA advisors,
who through their dedication and hard work have made a difference
in the lives of their students, and to the farmers of Kentucky, who
are as unique and diverse as the land on which they farm.

(Previous page photo submitted by Oneida Baptist Institute)

The Donning Company/Publishers
184 Business Park Drive, Suite 206
Virginia Beach, VA 23462

Steve Mull, General Manager
Dawn V. Kofroth, Assistant General Manager
Ed Williams, Project Director
Debbie Williams, Project Research Coordinator
Julia Kilmer-Buitrago, Senior Staff Writer
Jan Martin, Editor
Lori Wiley, Designer
John Harrell, Imaging Artist
Scott Rule, Senior Marketing Coordinator
Patricia Peterson, Marketing Coordinator

Library of Congress Cataloging-in-Publication Data

Barns of Kentucky / compiled by the Kentucky Future Farmers of America.
   p. cm.
  Includes index.
  ISBN 1-57864-144-6 (hard cover : alk. paper)
  1. Barns—Kentucky. 2. Vernacular architecture—Kentucky.   I. Future Farmers of
America. Kentucky Association.
  NA8230 .B269 2001
  728'.922'09769—dc21
                         2001032567

Printed in Hong Kong

CONTENTS

FOREWORD

The Burley Tobacco Growers Cooperative Association is proud to bring you *Barns of Kentucky*—a photographic journey through the landscapes of Kentucky. Kentucky is blessed with a variety of barns—tobacco barns, dairy barns, cattle and hay barns, horse barns, and a mixture of outbuildings. These structures tell stories about the people and the economy of the communities. Barns add a rich element to Kentucky's deep agricultural history. They tell a story of our way of life over the past years.

We are equally proud to sponsor this book for the Kentucky Future Farmers of America (FFA) Association. The FFA is easily considered one of the world's finest youth organizations. FFA members often become leaders in not only the agricultural industry, but in the world. The majority of the Burley Co-op's members were FFA members. We understand the strong importance of this organization and consider it an honor to work with the Kentucky FFA.

The Burley Tobacco Growers Cooperative Association represents 150,000 tobacco farmers and farming families in five states. Since 1941, we have administered the price support program and represented growers on both the state and national levels. We've watched and are watching our industry evolve with the times. But two things remain constant—the priceless farmland on which heritage and quality are grown and the strong farming families where pride and love is nurtured.

Kentucky's farming families, Kentucky's future farmers, and Kentucky's barns—Standing Strong.

Danny McKinney
Chief Executive Officer
Burley Tobacco Growers Cooperative Association
January 2001

INTRODUCTION

Webster's defines **barn** (bärn), *noun*, as a covered farm building for storing grain, hay, etc., and for stabling livestock; *verb transitive*, to store in a barn. This definition is a derivative of Old English words—*bere*, barley, and *ern*, a place—that literally mean "a place to store barley." Merely relying on this definition is to say that an apple is only an edible fruit and that the *Titanic* was just another boat, with no real regard or significance to their roles in history.

From the coal-filled mountains of Pike County to the Mississippi River bottoms of Fulton County, Kentucky has a very diverse agricultural community. Kentucky's agricultural products include tobacco, corn, soybeans, hay, cattle, hogs, horses, sheep, and other specialty crops and livestock too numerous to mention. The barns associated with each entity are diverse as well. Whether one is viewing the thoroughbred barns of the Lexington area from the interstate highways or traveling by some of the diary farms of the Louisville suburbs, we find ourselves absorbed into the beautiful surroundings often taken for granted.

The barn has been a mainstay in the history and evolution of the farm. From the meager beginnings of a grain-storing facility to the present modern-day works of engineering, the barn has been and continues to be an integral part of everyday agricultural life. The barns that dot the landscape throughout the Commonwealth of Kentucky are as unique and diverse as the regions in which they are located. Many have stood the test of Mother Nature and the test of time, and they continue to hold the unique histories associated with such events.

Having been blessed by being reared on my family's farm, I grew up around all types of farm buildings. Many times I went with my grandmother to help collect the hen eggs from the chicken house or to get a bucket of potatoes from the cellar. Each fall I would help my grandfather salt and hang the hams, shoulders, and middlings in the smokehouse, which was the oldest of the buildings, dating back to the 1800s, and was made from hand-hewed logs. My father helped to build two barns as he grew up on the farm, the most notable of which is a livestock barn built into the hillside. The head wall supporting the barn against the bank is made from chiseled sandstone rock, which my grandfather laid. We still drive and park equipment and store hay in the loft while feeding the livestock in the stalls underneath. The milk cows, mules, and pigs have long since been replaced by beef cattle in this unique barn, which is still the heart of the farm.

Beside almost every road and highway in Kentucky stands a barn. Many of the once new and proud structures have begun to show their age and the effects of time. Many of these barns now show the effects of more than a century's worth of wind, rain, and snow. They have sheltered freshly cut hay and tobacco throughout countless harvests, as well as been witness to the births of many foals, calves, and pigs, and let us not forget puppies and kittens! I sometimes wonder how many more seasons they will see. Will our next generation restore or build new barns and continue to dot the countryside?

As we now enter the twenty-first century, will the next several generations experience the beauty of farm life, just as many Kentuckians have in the past, or will the rural countryside give way to urban sprawl? Only the future knows. But for now, we can still take our leisurely drives down the back roads of Kentucky and experience the beauty of Mother Nature, and we can continue to see the handiwork of previous generations through the barns of Kentucky.

Douglas V. Wilson
Advisor
Jackson County Future Farmers of America

ACKNOWLEDGMENTS

This project has been a collaboration of agriculture students, FFA members, teachers, professors, farmers, and even a few professional photographers. They have spent over a year photographing, collecting, sorting, and selecting to get to this point.

A special thank you goes to Doug Wilson, whose tireless efforts in collecting photographs from around the state have made this book into a reality. Also, thanks to Ed Williams of The Donning Company Publishers for his commitment to the project and his willingness to see it through to the very end.

Heartfelt thanks go to all the FFA members, agriculture teachers, and supporters for providing the outstanding photographic work that is contained in this book. The dedication of the FFA shows that America's agricultural future is in very good hands.

Extreme thanks and gratitude go to the Burley Tobacco Growers Cooperative Association, Danny McKinney, CEO, and the Burley Co-op Board of Directors, whose generous financial support turned this dream into reality.

Most importantly, thanks go to all those whose dedication to agriculture provided this world with such marvelous pieces of agricultural architecture. This book is dedicated to all farmers everywhere.

TYPES OF BARNS

Barn architecture has become an increasingly popular area of study for historians. The design and size of a barn can tell a lot about the people who built it. Different needs and different cultural influences greatly determine the appearance of today's barns.

There are many different types of barns found throughout the United States. Although horse and tobacco barns count for most of the barns in Kentucky, other barns can be found throughout the countryside.

(Photo by Donald H. Scott)

English Barn   Also known as a Yankee barn, the English barn style was brought to the United States in the early to mid-1800s by immigrants from many different European countries (not just England). The main purpose of the English barn was grain processing or storage. It was often constructed with heavy timber, such as oak. The floor of an English barn was usually divided into three or more sections. The center section was used mainly for threshing grain such as wheat; the other sections were used for sorting and collecting the grain. Although extremely popular, with the invention of automated threshing machinery, the English barn quickly became obsolete.

German or Bank Barn   The German barn, also called the Sweitzer or bank barn, is possibly one of the oldest barn designs found in the United States. First built in the early 1700s, this style originally came from Switzerland. This barn usually had two levels, with the cattle on the ground floor and feed or hay on the upper loft. Many of these barns were built in the northeast against hillsides, so the farmer could directly enter the upper level from the hillside. In some of these barns built in Pennsylvania, a forebay, or a projection from the upper level, was built to provide a place for threshing. The grain could then be dropped to the animals from the forebay.

New England Barn   As the name suggests, the New England barn was popular in the New England region. Its design in many ways was similar to the English barn, only the center area was not designed for threshing. This barn was very popular because the center section could be lengthened to make a larger barn. Often this barn would be seen as part of a series of connected buildings that composed the farmstead. The house, workshop, barn, kitchen, and other outbuildings were all interconnected, a useful building technique for those cold New England winters.

(Photo by Donald H. Scott)

Dutch Barn   As Dutch immigrants began settling in the Hudson River Valley of northern New York state, the Dutch barn began to gain popularity. One of the easiest ways to spot a Dutch barn was the gabled roof, which sometimes would extend almost to the ground. Other common features were stock doors at each of the corners and horizontal clapboard siding. These building techniques worked to make a Dutch barn seem larger than it actually was in reality. These barns did not feature many openings, except for a center door with a small pent roof on the narrow side for wagons and a door to the stock aisles on both of the side ends.

Although impressive from the outside, the inside of the Dutch barn was even more overwhelming. Large beams were arranged in H-shaped units supported by columned aisles. At the end of the crossbeams, the columns were generally rounded to form "tongues," which was a style exclusive to the Dutch barns. Due to the massive amount of upkeep these barns have needed over the years, very few still survive today.

Prairie or Midwest Barn   As its name suggests, the Prairie barn was found mostly on the wide open plains of the Midwest. The main purpose of this barn is to feed and shelter cattle and other livestock and often this barn is long. This style of barn is believed to have been brought to the United States by German settlers who relocated throughout the Midwest in the post–Civil War era. One of the recognizable features of this barn is the peak roof that projects from a hayloft opening on the upper level. This style of barn is what most Americans think of when they think of a standard barn.

(Photo by Donald H. Scott)

Tobacco Barn   One of the two most common forms of barns in Kentucky is the tobacco barn. The tobacco barn is used primarily for the curing process of the tobacco plant. Tobacco leaves are hung on rails inside the barn and water evaporates from the leaves. Tobacco barns often have windows and air vents in the walls that can be opened and closed to help regulate humidity and temperature. The design and even the color of the barn are determined by the type of tobacco and its curing needs.

Kentucky Show Horse Barn   One of the more popular barn designs in central and northern Kentucky is the show horse barn. These barns are often built to comfortably house champion (or future champion) racing horses, and they require special attention to ventilation and drainage to keep a horse in top health condition. Unlike other forms of livestock barns, many of these show horse barns tend to be very ornamental in nature.

Round Barn   In the late 1880s, round barns began to increase in popularity as an economical alternative to the rectangular barns that had been used. The reasoning behind round barns was that cattle could be fed more easily by having a central silo. Also, the round shape was supposed to provide better ventilation and a lesser cost in building materials. The round shape provided increased stability and a self-supporting roof. Unfortunately, round barns seemed to be a challenge for carpenters of the time. While there are many true round barns, a number of multi-sided barns, which have 12 to 16 sides, were also built. Although round barns lost out to their rectangular counterparts in terms of popularity, they are often thought of as one of the more unique additions to the barn world.

Dairy Barn   Dairy barns, as the name suggests, are used to house dairy cattle and process milk. The dairy barn must be able to keep the cows warm, clean, and dry to help prevent illness in the cows or bacterial growth in the milk. A well-built dairy barn must be able to handle the heat and humidity generated by livestock through adequate ventilation. Dairy barns are still built in large numbers today, although many historical dairy barns also can be found throughout the country.

Pole Barn   Pole barns are a relatively new addition to the agricultural world. These barns resemble metal sheds and became popular after World War II. These new barns are used to house machinery instead of livestock or hay. Easy to assemble and relatively inexpensive, these barns have become a prominent addition to the farm world. As farms become more automated, pole barns will be used to house more equipment. A current trend is to have several small pole barns replace one large high-maintenance barn.

Crib Barn   Crib barns are found mainly throughout the South and southeastern United States, often in mountainous regions like the Appalachian and Ozark Mountains. Crib barns are used for both storage and smaller livestock, including pigs. These barns are built with a log cabin-like structure of unchinked logs and are sometimes covered with siding. Early crib barns had wood shingles, although they were quickly replaced with tin shingles. These tin shingles give the crib barn a nostalgic and rustic appearance. Six to eight crib stalls are usually located in these barns, with an aisle running between them.

Other Types of Barns   Many other types of barns can be seen throughout Kentucky and the United States. Many reflect the different cultural influences of the builders, including "threebay" English barns, Finnish log barns, or Czech house barns. Others reflect the building material available, such as adobe barns in California. Naturally, the barns reflect the needs of the region as well. In a livestock area, more horse and cattle barns were built than in an agricultural area. Some barns were built by land-grant universities, sold by mail order (such as Sears, Roebuck and Company), or built through work programs during the Depression.

Regardless of where they came from, these different styles of barns make interesting and historic additions to the countryside throughout America.

PURCHASE REGION

Located in the far western part of the state, the Purchase Region is settled on a gently rolling plain. Many major rivers flow nearby, including the Ohio, Mississippi, Tennessee, and Cumberland.

Located on Highway 68 three miles from the McCracken–Marshall County line in Marshall County near Sharpe, this barn was constructed in the late 1890s by Boone Hill to house dark tobacco. It was built from lumber off the farm that Boone Hill's grandfather homesteaded. Boone Hill was the first president of the West Kentucky Dark Fired Tobacco Association and held that office until 1966, four years before his death at age 94. The farm is now owned by his son-in-law, Dorse O'Dell, and his grandson, Kyle O'Dell. (Submitted by Kyle O'Dell)

This structure, constructed in 1950 with a concrete foundation and white oak framing, is located on the Lanny Fisk Farm at 851 Arant Road in Marshall County. The barn was constructed by H. Bert Smith, Roy Phelps, and Colvin Fisk. It has a feed room, five milking stalls, and a loft with 1,000-bale hay storage. Sliding doors have been added to the front, however, the tin roof and much of the siding is original.

In 1915, this barn, located at the Intersection of Highway 408 and Jackson School Road in Benton, Kentucky, was built by John Smith to accompany the house he had built around 1912. All construction on the barn was done by hand, although Mr. Smith did use his sawmill, located behind the barn, to make the lumber. The corner supports were hewn by hand and the foundation was made of creekstone. The barn, located on Mr. Smith's ninety-plus-acre farm, served as shelter for his horses and cows and as storage. The barn is now owned by his granddaughter, Kaye Oliver, and her husband, Kenny, who also reside on the farm. (Submitted by Michelle Portis)

Fourteen miles west of Paducah on Harris Road, this barn was built around 1914 by the Rudolph family. It was later renovated by Hubert Childress in 1974 when his family moved back to the old farmstead. This barn has continuously served as a haven for cattle and horses. In recent years, the barn has served as a place to store square bales of hay and equipment. (Submitted by Ronza D. Childress)

This barn was constructed in the late 1880s by Brother Duncan Long and is located ten miles west of Paducah on New Hope Road. It was used to store square bales of hay, farm implements, and, during winter months, it served as a shelter for horses and cattle. Today the barn serves as a place to store hay and medicate cattle, while the side sections house farm equipment. (Submitted by Ronza D. Childress)

This barn, located ten miles south of Paducah on Old Mayfield Road, was built in the fall of 1949 by Robert Goodwin and his family. It was used to store corn and square bales of hay and straw. It housed two horses, one milk cow, and sows and pigs in the winter. It is now used to store equipment and square bales of straw in the loft. The barn was repainted in 1995.

The Mabel Garrett Pullen Farm/Barn was renovated in 1996 by Murray State University (MSU) officials after it was bequeathed to MSU by Mrs. Pullen following her death in 1995. The farm was originally purchased by Stanley Pullen, the first chairman of MSU Agriculture, in the 1920s. He ran College Crest Farm with the help of students as employees, and their operation included a dairy. Mr. Pullen built the barn that still stands on the property, but he passed away in 1935 before the mortgage could be paid. Mrs. Pullen took many local teaching jobs to pay the mortgage. (Photo courtesy of Murray State University)

The Heathcott Rodeo Barn was built in 1997 and was named in honor of Dr. Eldon Heathcott, former chairman of MSU Agriculture and longtime MSU Rodeo Program supporter. The barn is used to board personally owned horses of Rodeo Program students. It has twenty-five stalls and was built with the help of supporters, such as Mr. and Mrs. Dan Evans of Bob Evans Restaurant, Inc. (Photo courtesy of Murray State University)

The farm's original name was the Tom Doran Farm, and A. F. "Bub" Doran built the barn between 1935 and 1940. Lamar Farmer used it to fire dark tobacco. Mr. and Mrs. Jackie Butterworth bought the farm around twenty-five years ago. In 1996 they built a new home on the property and decided to make the barn part of the driveway. They widened the doors and made it a "drive-through." (Photo courtesy of Murray State University)

Mr. Tom Wilkes built the barn in the mid-1930s, and it was used to fire dark tobacco until the mid-1980s. The barn/farm was bought by Otho and Sunshine Clark in the 1930s. In the old days the barn was fired with corncobs and hickory nut hulls. It caught on fire during the curing season several years ago, but Sunshine managed to extinguish the fire. The fourth generation of the Clark family is now being reared on the farm.

Built in the early 1900s, this barn has wooden pegs in its original structure. The sheds were added later. Originally built as a stock barn, it was later used as a tool shed and is now used to house burley tobacco.

This dairy barn is owned by Robert E. Elliott. Built in 1953, the barn is used for storing hay in the hayloft and for milking cows down below.

This pole barn was built in 1952 and has been used for storing hay, tractors, and trucks. Robert E. Elliott owns the barn.

Pete Carisle is the owner and builder of this barn, which was built in the late 1970s. It is used to store hay and keep horses.

Located at the intersection of Highways 131 and 80, this barn was built in the early 1990s. It is used to store hay, horses, and tack. The owner and builder is Pete Carisle.

This barn, built in the early 1900s, is owned by Bill Lattimer and is used for hay storage. There is a hall on each side for mules and the storage of buggys. It is located in a wooded area on Highway 166 just west of Fulton, Kentucky.

Harold Pewitt, son of the barn's original owner, Harvey Pewitt, now owns this barn that was built in the mid-1930s. It has a hayloft, corncrib, and stalls that were once used for keeping farming mules in at night and are now used for storing farm machinery. The barn, which was restored and covered with siding in 1999, is located on Highway 1706 three miles west of Fulton. (Photo by Donna Pewitt Garland)

This barn was built in the late 1800s and was owned by William Campbell, great-grandfather of the barn's current owner, Joe Forrest Campbell. The barn was built with hand-hewn poplar logs and was originally used as a milk barn; today the barn is used for storing hay. It is located five miles west of Fulton on Highway 781.

The Burnette Farms barn has been in the family since it was built in the early 1930s. It was originally owned by Cecil Burnette, who is the great-great-uncle of the current owner, Jeff Burnette, and his wife, Jean. The mural was painted by Jean's brother, Richard Pickle. The barn is located on Highway 94 four miles west of Fulton. (Photo by Jean Burnette)

Located two miles from Hickman on Highway 125, this barn was built in 1951 and was originally owned by James and Shirley Shaw. The current owners, Hal and Jill Coffey, added the brick in 1998 when they built their house. The barn is used for beef and dairy cattle. (Photo by David A. Black)

PENNYRILE REGION

This barn has captured the interest of many due to its arched gambrel-style roof. At the top center the roof continues its arch and does not reach a peak. It also is one of the few if not the only "bank" barns in the county. It is located on Dycusburg Road off Highway 641 in the Fredonia Valley. Upon further investigation, the style of the roof pales in comparison to the history of the structure.

The barn was first built in the 1880s, but no one can put a date on it. It was owned by the W. C. Rice and Co. Tobacco Stemmery Company and was used as a warehouse for the tobacco that was processed by the company. All the tobacco that was processed by the company was exported to Liverpool,

England. It is known from records that the company existed in 1893 and continued for at least fourteen more years. In November 1907, the Night Riders burned the main stemmery in Fredonia and also this warehouse. Only the foundation was left standing, as it was made of quarried limestone rock from the Fredonia Valley.

The foundation alone remained until approximately 1936 when a new owner of the property decided to place a roof over the foundation. No one knows why the style of the roof was chosen. This barn is a "bank" barn—one

may enter the loft from ground level at one end of the barn.

The second barn is a unique one in Caldwell County. It is the only Rock City barn in the county, and it's one of approximately 130 Rock City barns left in the United States. The owner reportedly still receives a check of approximately $45 annually for the advertisement on the barn, which is located on Highway 91 North.

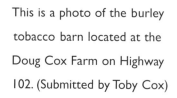

This is a photo of the burley tobacco barn located at the Doug Cox Farm on Highway 102. (Submitted by Toby Cox)

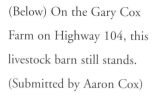

(Below) On the Gary Cox Farm on Highway 104, this livestock barn still stands. (Submitted by Aaron Cox)

The barley barn at the Allen Potter Farm on Potter Road once produced heat from a gas well on the farm. (Submitted by A. J. Potter)

the pennyrile region

by Julie P'Pool
Kentucky FFA President

Barns from 1940–1960 in Hopkinsville. (Photo by Mike Pyle)

The Pennyrile Region is made up of a great diversity in agriculture. The agriculture of the region consists of tobacco, corn, soybeans, wheat, beef and dairy cattle, and swine operations. The farms of the region consist mainly of family farms, but there has been an increase in the number of commercial farms.

The counties of the region are Webster, Livingston, Lyon, Caldwell, Crittenden, Trigg, Hopkins, Muhlenberg, Christian, and Todd. From one end of the region to the other, there are vast differences in areas of production. Throughout the region the crops are very similar but the livestock types change.

There is a great variance in the barns of the region. Driving through the area you can find tobacco barns and barns used to house livestock. Most of these barns are old and have been restored, while some of the older barns remain authentic to the time they were built. There have been many new barns built over the past few years. These are mainly used for tobacco, but some are used for livestock purposes.

Due to the high number of people involved with agriculture in the Pennyrile Region, FFA is an organization many youth become involved in. The region has approximately 1,200 members who participate in activities ranging from speaking contests to leadership conferences to livestock shows.

GREEN RIVER REGION

L
Located along the Indiana border, the Green River Region has had many significant floods within the past century.

This tobacco barn, owned by Bill Kuegel, is located on Highway 81 just outside of Owensboro, Kentucky. The barn was painted to advertise a local tobacco warehouse. Barn advertising is becoming a thing of the past in this area. (Submitted by the Apollo FFA)

This barn, built in the 1940s, is located eight miles southwest of Owensboro. The barn was painted by an Apollo High School graduate in the 1980s to advertise a tanning spa in Calhoun, Kentucky. The barn is owned by John Kuegel. (Submitted by the Apollo FFA)

During the flood of 1997, water surrounded this barn located on the Wahl Farm in the Birk City Community section of Daviess County. Backwater from the Green River caused flooding in the Hurricane Slough area. This photo was taken from a boat by Grady Ebelhar. Scott Paper Company buildings appear in the right-hand background. (Submitted by the Apollo FFA)

This tobacco barn, located at the Joe Foster Farm in Stanley, Kentucky, was built after the flood of 1937 on mounded ground along the Ohio River. The Foster family named their farm "Floodland Farms" due to the flooding from the river during heavy rains of the spring season. (Submitted by the Apollo FFA)

This is an old dairy barn located south of Sargo. The silo still has the roof on it, which is very unusual for an old silo. This barn is on land farmed by Kamuf Brothers Farms. (Submitted by the Apollo FFA)

This photo was taken during the flood of 1997 along Rhodes Creek, which is close to the Green River. Thousands of acres of Daviess County farmland stayed under water during early March of that year. This photo of the Harris Farm was taken by Grady Ebelhar from a boat. (Submitted by the Apollo FFA)

The Kenneth Ebelhar Farm in Birk City Community is shown in this photograph taken during the flood of 1997. Water has surrounded these barns three times since the first major flood in 1937. The photo was taken by Grady Ebelhar from a boat in March of 1997. (Submitted by the Apollo FFA)

This barn is located on the Joe Foster Farm along the Ohio River near Stanley, Kentucky. The barn was built in 1938 after the devastating flood of 1937. The ground was mounded to keep floodwater out of this barn. The Foster family has farmed this land since 1870. (Submitted by the Apollo FFA)

This barn on the Wimsatt Farm was built in the 1940s as an identical match to another barn on the cattle farm. This barn has a star cut in the front as a symbol of the builder. (Submitted by the Apollo FFA)

This barn was built by Tom Watson in 1930 and was used for hay on the cattle farm. The barn is very unique in design because it has no interior post in the loft. The tongue-and-groove floor of the loft supported the roof of the barn. (Submitted by the Apollo FFA)

This photo was taken after a snowfall in 1995. The tobacco barn is located on the Ruth Wimsatt Farm and the photo was taken by Grady Ebelhar. (Submitted by the Apollo FFA)

This barn is located in Whitesville, Kentucky, twelve miles east of Owensboro, Kentucky. The barn is seventy-five years old and was painted twenty years ago. The idea for the face came from a local man who thought it would be a unique idea. The Bible scriptures were put on to reflect the strong Christian beliefs in the community. The barn has been used for storage and as a tobacco barn, and it has become a landmark of the farm.

Located on Road 256 west of Calhoun and owned by W. T. Hull, this barn has been used for many years to store grain, mainly soybeans. (Submitted by the McLean County FFA)

This barn, owned by Clyde Dame and used for tobacco, is located on Park Creek Road. (Submitted by the McLean County FFA)

The barn shown here is owned by Jack Johnson and is used for tobacco. It is located in the Beech Grove area of Bonhannon Road off Beulah Church Road and 136 West. (Submitted by the McLean County FFA)

Located on Highway 81 south of Sacramento, Kentucky, this barn was owned by A. Whitemer and used for cattle and hay. (Submitted by the McLean County FFA)

Owned by Floyd DeLacy Farms, this barn is located on Highway 140 east of Glenville and is used for tobacco and mechanical storage. (Submitted by the McLean County FFA)

This barn is located on Highway 1046 south of Glenville,
Kentucky. It is owned by A. Roy Troutman, a tobacco
farmer. (Submitted by the McLean County FFA)

These are photos of a corncrib used in the late 1800s to the early 1900s. These corncribs were used for eared corn, which was thrown by scoop shovels through the small windows located on the sides. This particular crib is on concrete pillars and is on top of a rock mound to keep the wood and corn out of the backwater when the river rises. This crib is located on the edge of the Ohio River.

This is a tobacco barn that was occupied in the early 1900s. There are several layers of rafters in the center of this barn where tobacco was hung at different heights to be cured. This barn is located off Rockford Road in Uniontown.

This is a grocery store in the Uniontown Alzey Bottoms borderline of Union and Henderson Counties. This store sits high in the air on concrete blocks to stay out of the backwater. The '97 in white letters on the light pole shows how high the water rose in 1997. This building is located on Highway 136 outside of Smith Mills, Kentucky, near the Ohio River.

This is a barn that is still in use today as a machinery shed for farming equipment. This barn was built in the early 1900s and is located off of Highway 871 and Highway 360, three miles outside of Uniontown, Kentucky.

This barn is an old hay barn located off of Highway 871. There
are several old seed signs from years past posted on this barn.

This barn is located in Union County on the Charles
O'Nan Farm. This barn used to be an old mule barn.

This barn is on the Charles O'Nan Farm in Union
County. The small doors in the roof were used for "filling"
the barn with ear corn. It is used as a storage shed today.

This is a corncrib barn near the Ohio River.

Other barns reflect the
wide varieties of barns
available throughout the
Green River Region.

58

BARN ADVERTISING

During the 1950s Burma Shave advertisements drew the attention of many drivers around the country. These small signs would appear, one after another, along a road for travelers to read one line at a time. In rural regions, Burma Shave signs would have to compete with Mail Pouch Tobacco barn signs. Traveling painters would approach a farmer and ask him if they could paint a Mail Pouch advertisement on the side of his barn, usually with a small compensation for the farmer. One of the most common forms of compensation was painting the entire barn for the farmer at no cost, as long as he would permit one side to have the trademark Mail Pouch advertisement: "CHEW MAIL POUCH TOBACCO. TREAT YOURSELF TO THE BEST." In most cases this white lettering was painted on a black barn, although some red barns did exist. The black barn was ideal, since the tobacco barns were often painted black to assist in the tobacco-curing process. The last Mail Pouch painter hung up his brushes in 1992 after painting or repainting more than 20,000 barns. Although the tobacco advertisements have slowly drifted into memories, many people still paint unusual images on the sides of barns. Some images included in this book are a happy face, a Bible verse, and an open barn.

BARREN RIVER REGION

This 120-year-old barn belongs to Roger Buchanon and is located in northern Allen County in the community of Gainesville, Kentucky. The barn was built on farmland given to Citation Rigsby in 1810 as a land-grant for serving in the war. This land and barn have remained in the Buchanon family for seven generations. (Submitted by Georgiana Buchanon Fisher)

This barn is on the Wayne and Louise Shockley Farm in Allen County, located in the heart of Halifax, Kentucky. It was built by Ernest Smith around 1936 with lumber cut and sawed on the farm. There are eighteen-inch poplar boards in the barn doors. The barn is a combination livestock and feed barn. All of the original square posts remain in the barn, except for one that was knocked out by lightning.

This barn was built by Andy Joe Moore's great-great-grandfather in 1917 along the Barren River at 1630 Berry Store Road in Glasgow, Kentucky. It has a self-supporting roof with no posts in the loft. For years a hayfork was used to unload loose hay. The tracks are still located in the barn with the forks. Andy is a sophomore at Barren County High School. (Submitted by Joe M. Moore)

This old barn was built for the Harlin family in the 1890s by a well-known barn builder. This barn is located on the Kentucky–Tennessee border and is presently owned by the Comer family of Tompkinsville, Kentucky. In the 1920s the cedar-shingled roof was replaced with metal. Except for the doors, which were rebuilt, everything else is presently original.

This calf barn was built in the spring of 1999. The owner, Jason Holland, his father, Holly Holland, and Jerry and Jeremy Yokley built the frame and foundation and wired the barn. Jack Watson placed the metal sides and roof on the barn. The top is made of a woven multi-layer material supported by three-inch steel hoops that are fastened to 6" x 6" treated posts, all of which make the barn a 102' x 30' space used for housing baby calves. (Submitted by Corey Yokley)

This barn is located in Kentucky on the Allen–Monroe County line. It was built in 1996 by the owners, Paul and Joyce Hutchinson. The horse barn is constructed of a wood frame, metal siding, and a metal roof. The barn originally was 150' x 65' and now has a 50' x 26' shed attached. The barn consists of fourteen stalls and it has a walker and a ring. It is equipped for washing and breeding purposes. (Submitted by Corey Yokley)

This barn was built in 1962 by Robert Eaton. It was originally built from block. Metal was used to cover the barn in 1995 by builder Eddie Burgess. The barn is used for hay and feed and is presently owned by Freddie Hale of Fountain Run, Kentucky. (Submitted by Corey Yokley)

This 48' x 50' barn was built in the early 1900s by a contractor named Wart Biles. The foundation was formed from the large ground rock, the seals were made from logs, and the structure was built from chestnut wood. The side shed was added in the middle 1900s and repairs were done with poplar wood. The barn was recently painted and repairs were done on the inside. It is presently owned by a Holman Mennonite family from Michigan. (Submitted by Corey Yokley)

The livestock barn built in 1940 by Dr. W. A. Neely is the only one of its kind in Simpson County. The barn is owned by James Gann. The loft has no poles for support and is only supported by the rafters. All livestock are fed from a door opening in the floor to the livestock below. The floor can hold a tractor-trailer. (Submitted by David Duncan)

This dairy barn belongs to the Rice brothers. The barn was built in 1943 by Howard Hall. Mr. Hall wanted a functional dairy barn with access to easy feeding and easy-to-handle hay. He also wanted a barn unique to the area. (Submitted by David Duncan)

The livestock barn that belongs to Robert Hyde was built in 1860. It is one of the oldest standing barns in Simpson County. It has square nails and round wooden pegs holding the crossties and support poles. (Submitted by David Duncan)

The livestock and tobacco barn owned by Joe Richards, located on Gold City Road in Franklin, Kentucky, was built in 1930. Compared to other barns in the county, this barn is different because of its roof line. (Submitted by David Duncan)

Brad Kelley built his multipurpose live-stock barn in 1993. The barn is an all-steel building with steel beams, sides, and roof. (Submitted by David Duncan)

Located ten miles north of Bowling Green on Louisville Road, this small shed is owned by Charles Robertson of Bowling Green. The mural was painted by Lori James of Bowling Green. (Submitted by Dan Costellow)

This horse barn, owned by Dr. Fred Carter, is located off Louisville Road about seven miles north of Bowling Green. The mural was painted in 1991 by Lori James of Bowling Green. (Submitted by Dan Costellow)

This is the main horse barn on Ironwood Farm. It was built in 1989 and was designed by famed architect Benjamin Page of Nashville, Tennessee. It is located just north of Bowling Green, Kentucky, on Old Richardson Road. (Submitted by Dan Costellow, photo by David Garvin)

As if a statement of the tobacco business, this Kentucky tobacco barn has fallen into disrepair and desolation. Located on a farm near Beech Bend Park in Bowling Green, it is formerly owned by Charles Garvin and is now owned by Dallas Jones. (Submitted by Dan Costellow, photo by David Garvin)

This is an old barn located on Garvin Lane near Bowling Green, Kentucky, and is owned by Lillian Warner. (Submitted by Dan Costellow, photo by David Garvin)

This is an old barn known as the "Party Barn," where cook-outs, fish frys, and the like are held. It is located behind David Garvin's home on Ironwood Farm in Bowling Green, Kentucky. (Submitted by Dan Costellow, photo by David Garvin)

This is an old barn on the former farm of Elvis Donaldson, now owned by David Garvin. Some of the main beams in this barn came from a steamboat that sunk near the site at the old Bowling Green Boatlanding. (Submitted by Dan Costellow, photo by David Garvin)

Above: This is an old cattle barn that was built around the turn of the century by Roy Cooksey, Sr. It is located on Beech Bend Road near Bowling Green, Kentucky. (Submitted by Dan Costellow, photo by David Garvin)

Franklin Hogue's barn in Allen County is a combination tobacco, hay, live-stock, and machinery storage barn. (Courtesy of the Allen County FFA)

Horse barn on the Orville Clark Farm in Allen County, built in the 1980s. (Courtesy of the Allen County FFA)

Located on Hickory Ridge Road in Grafenburg, Franklin County, this barn is owned by Ray Richardson. (Photo by Kim Brinegar)

(Submitted by the Metcalfe County FFA)

(Submitted by the
Metcalfe County FFA)

This Ranchero-style Spanish-theme barn, which is adjacent to a house of the same style, is located in the heart of Butler County in the city of Morgantown. Living quarters and a pool table can be found in the upper level of the barn. The "Hacienda de las Colemans" is owned by Christine and Denzel Coleman. (Submitted by the Butler County FFA)

This barn is located in the heart of Rochester. (Submitted by the Butler County FFA and Ben Annis, agriculture teacher)

This barn was built by Ira Woodcock and was used to trade, break, feed, and groom his horses. Named the Blue "Dick" Stables, this barn is well known from Morgantown to Indianapolis. Mr. Woodcock recently passed away, but the barn still stands. (Submitted by the Butler County FFA and Ben Annis, agriculture teacher)

Randy Tabor's farm in Allen County has this combination horse-
training and hay storage barn. (Courtesy of the Allen County FFA)

Built in the early 1900s, this barn was used more yester-
year than last year. It is located on Dumont Hill in
Scottsville, Kentucky. (Courtesy of the Allen County FFA)

Located in Logansport, Kentucky, this barn is one of the largest in the area. It is owned by Loretta Moore. (Submitted by the Butler County FFA)

This barn's primary use is to feed horses, but it also has a side shed that is used to house tobacco. The barn is owned by Electa Annis and is located in Logansport. (Submitted by the Butler County FFA)

This barn was built around the turn of the century. Remodeled in the 1940s by Forest Miller, it is scheduled to be remodeled again in the near future. The barn features uniquely crafted stables and troughs and is used for boarding. (Submitted by the Butler County FFA)

This barn is owned by Weymouth Martin and is located on Logansport Road. (Submitted by the Butler County FFA)

The barn in this beautiful postcard setting is owned by Glendon Johnson. (Submitted by the Butler County FFA)

This barn was built in the early 1960s by Roy Johnson and is currently owned by Richard and J. P. Rogers. It is located on the infamous Reeds Ferry Road, which is home to one of the last county-operated ferry boats in Kentucky. (Submitted by the Butler County FFA)

the color of barns

If you ask the average person what color a barn should be, the usual answer is red. Traditionally, many barns throughout the United States have been painted red, although the reason behind this color choice has been somewhat disputed. Some say that the red color was used because it was fairly inexpensive, due to the inclusion of ferrous oxide (rust) for coloration. Another less popular theory says that the red barns were used to simulate brick, a sign of wealth among certain groups.

In Kentucky, however, one color for barns seems to stand out from the rest. That color is black. Although other states have black barns, Kentucky seems to have more of them than any other state.

The black color is not just for its timeless class, however. Kentucky barns, especially tobacco barns, are dressed in black for practical reasons. One reason that has been suggested for the black coloring again has to deal with the cost of pigmentation. By using lamp black and diesel fuel as an inexpensive wood preservative, farmers could protect the barn structures with the least cost.

A more likely reason for the black coloration has to do with the tobacco curing process. A black barn absorbs more heat than another color, which speeds up the drying process. Since it takes a couple months to dry and cure the tobacco, any way to speed up the process is welcome. Once the tobacco is harvested, it is hung inside the long black barns that have doors for ventilation. Although this makes sense, Kentucky has a large number of horse barns that also are painted black. In addition, some farms have black fences and other black buildings to match the black barns. Perhaps these barns retain their black color as a tribute to the agricultural base that tobacco provided to the young commonwealth.

Regardless of the reason behind Kentucky's black barns, their black coloring has become a Kentucky tradition in many counties. Still, other colors can be found throughout Kentucky's countryside, including white, green, yellow, blue, and natural wood coloring. Down almost any rural road, a traveler is sure to see a Kentucky barn. Although the colors may vary, the durability and dedication to Kentucky agriculture remain constant.

LINCOLN TRAIL REGION

The burley in this barn will cure well because the barn sits on the "Breaker of the Bluegrass," which lines the northeast end of Hardin County. The "Breaker of the Bluegrass" is the geographic change one notices when heading east on the Bluegrass Parkway from Elizabethtown. (Submitted by Lloyd A. Horne)

This sixty-year-old barn is different because of its construction. This barn was built with a completely self-supporting roof. The absence of posts and support beams allowed the barn's owners, the Millers, to move and handle loose hay more efficiently. (Submitted by Lloyd A. Horne)

This tobacco barn on the Miller
Farm is ready for the burley. The
stripping room on the side of the
barn is no longer being used. With
the advent of stripping boxes, the job
had to be moved to larger spaces.
(Submitted by Lloyd A. Horne)

The silo sits ready as the corn matures on the left. This stock barn enables the Millers to finish feeding calves after they are weaned.

This barn off the Bluegrass Parkway towards New Haven, Kentucky, was designed in the early 1900s as a milking barn, hay barn, animal shelter, and tool shed all in one. Today the barn is used to house equipment and, on occasion, tobacco. (Submitted by Stacy K. Vincent)

This small livestock barn is located outside of the Boston community. The barn shown here is a sample of what most rural Kentucky barns followed. This building allows livestock to have an area for shelter and rest. (Submitted by Stacy K. Vincent)

This double-four milking parlor allows Jeff Lewis
and Rob Walker of Sunshine Dairy outside of
Bloomfield, Kentucky, to milk over one hundred
heads twice a day. The barn was renovated last
fall. (Submitted by Stacy K. Vincent)

NORTHERN KENTUCKY REGION

The J. H. Conrad Drover Barn, owned by Tony Brewer, is one of the oldest working cattle barns in Northern Kentucky. During the late 1800s and early 1900s (prior to 1940), it was used as a stop-over area for cattle to rest and receive hay and water while on their way to market in Cincinnati. It was recognized as a Kentucky historical site and certified by Governor Paul Patton.

The tobacco barn owned by Joe
Gruen is one of the largest barns in
Grant County—the barn is seven
tiers high. It is located on the
south side of Dry Ridge, Kentucky.

This large dairy barn was built in the 1940s by Perry Gaines, who operated a large milk-processing and delivery business in the area. It is located on Highway 42 north of Carrollton and is currently owned by Dow Corning Inc. (Submitted by Ed Nelson, agriculture instructor at Carroll County High School)

This very large dairy barn was built for A. B. Dunn in the 1920s. It is located on Highway 55 south of Carrollton and is currently owned by Floyd and Sandy Shamblin. This barn is now being used for horses. (Submitted by Ed Nelson, agriculture instructor at Carroll County High School)

This very large dairy barn was built in 1944 to replace the original that was built in the 1920s. Both barns were built by R. M. Barker of Richlawn Farm. The unique roof style is made from a solid one-piece truss design. This barn is located on Highway 42, just northeast of Carrollton, and has been completely restored by the current owner, Atofina Chemicals, Inc. (Submitted by Ed Nelson, agriculture instructor at Carroll County High School)

This unusual barn was built by R. M. Barker of Richlawn Farm in the 1920s for Duroc hogs. The center of the structure contains a ring for showing hogs. The barn is located just northeast of Carrollton on Highway 42 and has been completely restored by the current owner, Atofina Chemicals, Inc. (Submitted by Ed Nelson, agriculture instructor at Carroll County High School)

This dairy barn was built in 1946 by R. C. Caldwell and his son-in-law, W. T. Nelson, to replace the original barn that had burned. The unique round roof style was made by bending green oak lumber. Current use of the barn includes beef cattle and alfalfa hay. The barn is located on Salt Creek Road south of Bethlehem and is owned by Mr. Caldwell's grandson, Ed Nelson. (Submitted by David Stahl, agriculture instructor at Henry County High School)

This barn was originally built from logs in 1850 for Judge Pryor's cattle, and it was remodeled in 1950 by the current owner, Rex Prather. Remodeling involved lifting of the original barn and adding a lower story of concrete blocks for hogs. The barn is located on Highway 421 in New Castle. It is currently being used as a woodworking shop by Rex Prather. (Submitted by David Stahl, agriculture instructor at Henry County High School)

This barn was built by Mal Orem in 1919 for mules. The build date and Orem name are engraved in the front roof's vent spire. It is located on Orem Lane east of Campbellsburg and is currently owned by Duane McManis. (Submitted by David Stahl, agriculture instructor at Henry County High School)

KENTUCKY STATE FACTS AT A GLANCE

The origin of the name Kentucky is a source of much controversy. Some suggest that the name Kentucky has two possible origins from the Iroquois: "Ken-tah-ten," meaning land of tomorrow or dark and bloody ground; others say that it comes from a Cherokee word for the area south of the Ohio River that means "meadowland."

Kentucky, which joined the United States on June 1, 1792, was the fifteenth state in the Union and is one of four states that calls itself a commonwealth.

State Flag: The state seal is centered on a blue field and was approved by the General Assembly in 1928. Kentucky's first flag is displayed at the Kentucky History Museum in Frankfort.

State Seal: Two friends embracing with the state motto encircling them. Authorized in 1792, the state motto is believed to be from a Revolutionary War song called "The Liberty Song," which was a favorite of Kentucky's first governor, Isaac Shelby.

Capitol: **Frankfort**

Largest City: **Louisville**

Population: **Just under 4,000,000**

Size: **Approximately 40,000 square miles and 37th state in land size**

Number of Counties: **120**

Highest Point: **Black Mountain**

State Motto: United We Stand, Divided We Fall

State Nickname: The Bluegrass State

State Flower: Goldenrod

State Tree: Tulip Poplar (Changed from the Coffee Tree in 1994)

State Bird: Cardinal

State Butterfly: Viceroy Butterfly

State Fish: Kentucky Spotted Bass

State Mineral: Coal

State Rock: Kentucky Agate

State Fossil: Brachiopod

State Gemstone: Freshwater Pearl

State Horse: Thoroughbred

State Wild Animal: Grey Squirrel

State Arboretum: Bernheim Arboretum and Research Forest

State Soil: Crider Soil Series

State Bluegrass Song: "Blue Moon of Kentucky"

State Song: "My Old Kentucky Home" by Stephen Foster

LICKING RIVER REGION

This barn was constructed in the late 1800s and was used for the production of Black Angus cattle. It has a hay manger that runs the length of the barn. The construction is mortise and tenon. Today it is used for hay storage and tobacco and is on the farm of Jim and John Rice. (Submitted by Terry Prather)

This barn was built in the early 1900s for the housing of tobacco and is located on the farm of Benny Cracraft. The construction is mostly mortise and tenon and yellow poplar was used throughout. The barn was painted by Harley Warrick and is near a main road. (Submitted by Terry Prather)

This barn is on the Herbert Porter Farm. It was built in 1800 and was used as a distillery and for the storage of hay. It is made of solid brick with holes in the sides and ends for timber frame construction. (Submitted by Terry Prather)

This barn is on the farm of Everett Hilterbrand. It was built in 1920 to house mules and it has ten sides and two stories. The mules are loaded into each side (holds ten) and fed from the upper level in the center so that all can be fed at once. (Submitted by Terry Prather)

The tobacco barn in the picture above was built in
the 1960s and is one of the largest in Montgomery
County. It is owned by Samuel "Mort" Havens and is
located on Tipton Road. The barn is ten bents long and
seven tiers high, and it will hold 700 rails of tobacco
when completely full. (Submitted by Alton Stull)

The Ellington barn is made of logs, which were constructed without nails. It has wooden pegs to hold the logs in place. It is said to be one of the oldest structures in Bath County. The barn is located on a farm that has been owned by David Ellington and his family dating back to 1838, but it is believed to have been owned longer than that. The barn was supposedly built in 1792. The farm where the barn is located is a sesqui-centennial farm in Kentucky. (Submitted by Jimmie Walton)

licking river

By Amanda Applegate
Kentucky FAA Treasurer

In the Licking River Region of Northern Kentucky, 80 percent of the barns have a multi-purpose use starting in the fall of each year. Tobacco storage is the primary use for August, September, October, and November, with a secondary use of storage for equipment underneath the tobacco. Once the tobacco is processed and delivered to market, the barns then have a use for cattle as well as more machinery. The other 20 percent of the barns are mainly cattle only, pertaining to dairy cattle.

Barns are a valuable asset to all farmsteads in this region of Kentucky. Walk in any given barn at any given time and not only will you find machinery, tobacco, and cattle, you also will find gardening tools, lawn care tools, family antiques, antique machinery, and many items from a family's past generations that they just can't seem to part with. It may look like junk, but to the owner it is a whole lot more.

tobacco processing

Unlike many other crops, tobacco is not taken directly from the field to the consumer. Tobacco must go through an extensive curing process before it is ready for market.

After tobacco is planted, it takes approximately five months for it to reach maturity. During that time, special attention must be taken to ensure that the plant does not succumb to blue mold, tobacco horn worm, or other ailments. Once the tobacco plants reach maturity, the leaves begin to droop toward the ground, signifying that the plant is ready for harvesting. This usually happens around late August.

First a tobacco plant is impaled on a spear and cut with a tobacco knife. This process is called "spiking." Each spear usually holds about six tobacco plants. The cut tobacco dries in the field for a day or so, depending on the weather, and then is taken to the barn on a scaffold wagon. This backbreaking work is made more difficult by the hot weather typical for that time of year. Without the hot weather, however, the curing process would not be possible.

Once the tobacco reaches the barn, each spear of the spiked tobacco is hung in a carefully planned order. Many times the tobacco is hung up two or three stories high in forty- to fifty-pound bundles. Once the barn has been completely loaded, hardwood slab and sawdust smoke fires are lit to begin the curing process. Tobacco curing can take several weeks or more. Once the leaves change color to a light or moderate brown, the curing process is complete. After the curing comes the stripping and then the tobacco is ready for market auctions. There is little time for a tobacco farmer to relax, however. Preparations must be made for next year's tobacco crop.

Kentucky's temperate climate provides a suitable environment for the production of tobacco. As a result, many farmers rely at least partially on their income coming from tobacco production. Tobacco accounts for more than one-third of Kentucky's net agricultural income. Somewhat surprising is the fact that 90 percent of the tobacco-growing farms in Kentucky grow less than ten acres of tobacco. Since tobacco can strip the land of its nutrients, farmers must constantly rotate other crops, such as corn, soybeans, or wheat, onto the land. The high market value of tobacco makes it possible for farmers to turn a profit on small parcels of tobacco farmland, which is why tobacco farming is such an integral part of Kentucky agriculture today.

BIG SANDY RIVER REGION

The Burton tobacco barn was constructed in the late 1800s of hewn beams and wooden pegs. In its early life the barn could house ten acres of tobacco. After many years, the barn continues to stand strong and proud, playing an important role in the time-honored tradition of producing a crop of the golden leaf, burley tobacco. The barn is located at Tar Kiln Farm, the home of the Ronald Burton family, 468 Tar Kiln Hill Road, Grayson, Kentucky, in Carter County.

A tobacco barn built in the early 1900s, this barn stands alone on a high point where the prevailing winds can reach unobstructed. The extra ventilation at the top allows for better air movement.

Signs of the times—silos at the rear of the barn have become overgrown with vines since the owner has discontinued feeding silage to his cows.

It all began in the early 1880s on a little creek in Johnson County, now known as Williams Creek, located near Flat Gap, Kentucky. One of the residents of that area, Stanford J. Williams, built a one-room schoolhouse on a small portion of his property so that the children of that area could begin their education. The building was constructed of yellow poplar logs that were cut and hauled from nearby hillsides. Each log was hewed to its near perfection with a broadax, even the flooring boards.

The little school closed its doors to education approximately seventy-five years ago. Then it was dismantled by Albert Williams (born April 18, 1885–died June 17, 1950), a son of the school's builder, Sanford J. Williams. Albert used the logs and flooring from the schoolhouse to build this barn, which has been used to house tobacco, hay, and livestock.

At Albert's death, the property was passed on to his youngest son, Sanford Sherwood Williams. Sherwood owned the property until his death in January 2000, then it was deeded to his daughter, Sharon Williams McCarty. The barn is still standing today and is used to house tobacco.

The logs that were used in building the main structure of the barn were cut from stumps approximately 115 years ago. (Submitted by Sharon McCarty)

This barn was constructed in the mid-1940s during the time when U.S. 23 was being built. An older barn had to be removed from the road site. J. H. Blackburn used part of the lumber from the older barn to build the newer one. After J. H. Blackburn died, the property on which he had built this barn was inherited by his daughter Mary Emma. This property was sold to Mark Ratliff in the spring of 2000. (Submitted by Mark Ratliff)

This barn was built in the early 1930s from hemlock spruce grown and sawed on the farm. The mill was owned by Marvin Sparks, and the barn was built by Marvin and John West Moore. The foundation was built out of red oak with two-by-fours, and the flooring and frame were built out of hemlock. The barn is two stories high for storing hay that was hauled in loose. Mangers were built on both sides to feed forty brood cows; the mangers hold forty squared bales each. Six individual stalls with feeding troughs and mangers were built for the work mules. (Submitted by Carolyn Jean Sparks)

history of the FFA

The Future Farmers of America (FFA) is a national organization that
promotes agricultural education among America's youth. The FFA was started
in 1920 by Henry Groseclose, an agricultural education instructor from
Blacksburg, Virginia. Within a few years other groups were established throughout the United States. Many of these programs were assisted by the Smith-
Hughes National Vocational Education Act of 1917, which established vocational agriculture courses nationwide.

Some of the agricultural activities for America's youth included the
New Farmers of America (NFA) for African-American boys, formed in 1926,
and the inclusion of youth at the American Royal Livestock Show, also in 1926.

Two years later in 1928, a group of thirty-three students from eighteen
states met at the National Livestock Judging Contests and decided to establish
the Future Farmers of America organization. Leslie Applegate of New Jersey
was elected president, and dues were set at ten cents per year. A main goal
of the Future Farmers of America was, and still is, to provide leadership
training for high school students of vocational agriculture.

As the membership grew, more FFA members began to attend the
national conventions, which were held in Kansas City, Missouri. In 1929, the
official colors—national blue and corn gold—and creed were adopted. The
blue corduroy jacket with the FFA emblem on the back was adopted in 1933
after a group from Fredericktown, Ohio, wore similar matching jackets to the
national convention. That same year members celebrated the first National
FFA Day. Fifteen years later, National FFA Day would become FFA Week,
celebrated to coincide with George Washington's birthday in honor of his
contributions to American agriculture.

The FFA grew considerably throughout the United States in its first
decade. By 1934 the FFA had chartered associations in forty-eight states.
(Rhode Island would charter its first association in 1950, followed by Alaska

in 1976.) With such great nationwide participation, national leadership was required. To support the growing organization, the National FFA Foundation, Inc., was established in Washington, D.C., in 1944. Its purpose was to raise money from corporate, individual, and government sponsors to support FFA programs nationwide. By 1948 the FFA had grown to be an international success through an international exchange with the Young Farmers Club of the United Kingdom.

Congress showed its support for the FFA in 1950 when it issued a Federal Charter and Recognition through the Department of Education. Three years later, the U.S. Post Office issued a special stamp to commemorate the FFA's silver anniversary. To help celebrate this milestone, President Eisenhower addressed the National FFA Convention.

In 1959, the FFA established its national headquarters in Alexandria, Virginia. Six years later, during the tumultuous years of the civil rights movement, the FFA merged with the New Farmers of America, adding 50,000 members and crossing the color barrier. Women were included in the national membership in 1969, which gave them the ability to hold office and participate in regional and national competitions.

To show support for its growing alumni, the National FFA Alumni Association was founded in 1971. A little more than a decade later, in 1988, middle school students were offered memberships for the first time.

In 1999, the national convention moved from Kansas City to Louisville, Kentucky. The convention had been held in Kansas City since the first convention in 1928. The National FFA Convention will be held in Louisville at least until 2005.

With its proud history and focus on the future, FFA is ensured a place in American life as one of the country's premiere youth programs and a friend to agriculture.

KENTUCKY RIVER REGION

This small barn was constructed in the 1950s and is primarily used for storing corn. It is currently owned by Billy Whitaker. (Submitted by the Rockcastle County FFA)

This barn is owned by Sylvia Leroy. It was constructed in the early 1900s and was primarily used to house tobacco. (Submitted by the Rockcastle County FFA)

This barn was constructed in 1955 and remodeled in 1993. It is currently owned by Judy and Roy Adams and is primarily used for horses. (Submitted by the Rockcastle County FFA)

This small barn was constructed in the late 1800s and was primarily used for livestock and hay. It is currently owned by Karen and Tony Ackerman. (Submitted by Helen and Darrell Whitaker of the Rockcastle County FFA Alumni)

This is Eastern Kentucky University (EKU) Stateland Dairy as it appeared prior to 1960. EKU began a relationship with the dairy industry in 1912 that continues today. No photos remain of the original site. The location shown in this photo is where the university's Alumni Coliseum now stands. Under the direction of A. B. Carter, Stateland Dairy, along with the University of Kentucky Dairy Farm and Berea College, were recognized nationally as dairy industry leaders during this era.

This is Eastern Kentucky University Stateland Dairy as it appeared from 1960 to 1996. Located adjacent to the campus, it was typical of dairy barns of this period. Hundreds of students remember being trained to milk in this facility. Campus expansion forced its relocation to Meadowbrook Farm in 1996.

This tobacco barn converted into a cattle feedlot is located in Clay County, Kentucky, on the Oneida Baptist Institute Farm. Oneida is a Christian boarding school for grades 6–12, and the students come from all over the world to attend. Beef for the school is produced in the feed-lot. The work is done by students enrolled in the agricultural programs. (Submitted by Oneida Baptist Institute)

This barn is located on Kentucky 472 in the Langnau community of Laurel County and is owned by the Tom Cornett family. It was built in 1947 by Billy Wyatt, Milford Wyatt, Raymond Wyatt, Hairm Cornett, Tom Cornett, and Les Hubbard. The barn was built strictly as a tobacco barn and is still used for that purpose. As of the year 2000, it has held fifty-three crops of tobacco. The barn is 120 feet in length and 60 feet wide; a shed was added in 1981 to accommodate more tobacco.

This barn is located on Raccoon Creek in Laurel County and belongs to Delford McKnight. It was built in the late 1980s and is presently used as a livestock barn. A hay-feeding shed is attached to the left rear of the barn.

This barn is located on Maplesville Road in Laurel County and is owned by Vada Owens. The barn was built in the early 1960s as a tobacco barn. It originally had a stripping room attached to the left side, but it was removed when high winds moved the entire barn off its original foundation. The barn is 60 by 40 feet.

These barns are located on Kentucky 472 near the Rockcastle River in eastern Laurel County. They were built in the mid-1940s by John P. Johnson. The one in the foreground was built strictly as a tobacco barn and the one in the background as a dairy and hay barn. The dairy barn was later converted to house tobacco. The present owner is Frank Cornett.

This is the new feed barn and manure stack pad that was built in 2000 on Harlos Wilson's farm. It feeds thirty heads of weaned beef calves. The barn is located in the Grassy area of Jackson County. (Photo by Daniel and David Wilson)

This barn is located in the Maplesville section of Laurel County. It belongs to J. T. "Tully" Owens and is used for housing tobacco and for square-bale hay storage. It was built in the early 1960s by Tully Owens.

The Oneida Baptist Institute, located near Oneida, was founded in 1899 and focuses on building character, with agriculture playing a fundamental role in helping shape the lives of youth.

This is the new feed barn and stack pad on Harry Wilson's farm. It was built in 2000 and feeds up to fifty heads of cattle. This barn was constructed with logs harvested from the farm, which has been in the family since the early 1830s. (Photo by Alexander Wilson)

This is the Bingham family's farm barn. It is used for tobacco, hay, corn, milking dairy cows, and weaning calves. (Photo by Candrea Bingham)

This barn on Riley Bingham's farm is used for tobacco and was built in the early 1980s. (Photo by Brian Bingham)

This turn-of-the-century tobacco barn is a ghost barn. It is located on Highway 421 in Egypt, Kentucky. (Photo by George Ferrell)

This red barn is used for livestock. It is located on Disputanta Road in Rockcastle County, near the towns of Big Hill and Morrill. (Photo by George Ferrell)

This multipurpose barn is used for hay, tobacco, and livestock. It is located on McCammon Ridge Road, south of McKee. (Photo by George Ferrell)

This tobacco and hay barn is near the site where Daniel Boone and others caught up with the band of Indians who had kidnapped Boone's daughter and another young girl from Boonesboro, Kentucky. The barn is located south of McKee at Indian Creek on Highway 89. (Photo by George Ferrell)

This tobacco barn is over seventy years old and is located on Highway 421 in Egypt, Kentucky. (Photo by George Ferrell)

This is another old tobacco barn located on Indian
Creek south of McKee. (Photo by George Ferrell)

This is an old tobacco barn with a side shed. It is located at the intersection of Highways 1953 and 1956, north of Sand Gap. (Photo by George Ferrell)

LAKE CUMBERLAND REGION

This tobacco stock barn, located on Watsun Chapel Road in eastern Casey County, was constructed in 1921 for $150. The owner, Clyde Foster, turned ninety years old in December 2000. This barn has been in his family his entire life, and he still walks to it daily to milk his Jersey cow. The barn is built from black oak lumber with boards on the shed in a bias pattern. In 1964, Clyde sold a tobacco crop for $2,600 and purchased a 1964 Ford Galaxy that he still owns today. (Submitted by Lauren Price)

This barn is set in the community of Gosser Ridge on Highway
3525 in Russell County. It was built in the early 1920s and has a
rock foundation and a wood-shingled roof. It was used as a stock
barn with six stables and a crib to hold corn. Two of the stables were
for horses and the other four were for cows that supplied milk for the
family. Tobacco was hung in the barn along with hay in the barn's
loft. This barn was laid to rest in 1992. (Photo by Linda M. Helm)

In the early 1990s, the Adair County Board of Education purchased approximately seventy acres that adjoined existing school property. A new high school was constructed in 1993, and a new agriculture facility was added shortly thereafter on the property. Like many farms in Kentucky, the land had a tobacco quota. FFA members at the time were eager for the opportunity to grow and sell the tobacco as a learning experience. Since then, the FFA tobacco crop has become a valuable learning experience for its members. Students are responsible for all aspects of the crop, including growing transplants, cultivation, planting, tilling, harvesting, and marketing. Each year a banquet is held for the chapter's 200-plus members and parents. The banquet is fully funded by the students' hard-earned tobacco money. (Photo courtesy the Adair County FFA)

This barn is located in the Coburg community of Adair County. It sits very near to where the Adair, Taylor, and Green county lines meet. It is also located within a few feet of the Central and Eastern Time Zone division line. The burley tobacco crop beside the barn will soon be ready for harvest. It will then be hung on the barn's tier rails for curing. (Photo courtesy of the Adair County FFA)

This barn is located in the White Oak community of Adair
County. The once green tobacco hanging in the barn has
turned golden brown and will soon be ready for stripping.
The side doors on the barn allow for more air circulation
and faster curing. The farmer may be lucky enough to have
his tobacco stripped and ready for sale before the cold
weather sets in. (Photo courtesy of the Adair County FFA)

This barn also is located in the White Oak community. It is sided with metal, which prevents air circulation. Vents in the roof allow dangerous heat to escape;
however, tobacco cured in this barn will have a darker
color, which is attractive to many buyers. This barn,
like many others in Kentucky, may house machinery,
hay, and even cattle during the tobacco off-season.
(Photo courtesy of the Adair County FFA)

This barn is located in Green County at 361 Sam Loyall Road.
The 204-acre farm has been in the Loyall family since the 1850s.
This barn was built in the early 1900s with the help of friends
and family of Lewis Loyall. This barn is 100 feet long and 80 feet
wide with a peak of 50 feet. Someone said (this quote has been
passed down), "It took 100 squares of metal to cover the barn."
This barn was built with five different loft levels. It also has a
track that is used to fill the loft full of hay.

This is the largest barn known to exist in Green County. It
has the capacity to handle fifty mules at a time. The barn was
well known as a breeding and trading area for horses and mules
and also has been used for cattle and hogs. The owner of the
farm, Nancy Loyall, resides on the farm. (Photo by Nancy Loyall)

lake cumberland

by Brandon K. Davis

Kentucky FFA Sentinel

The Lake Cumberland region is nestled in the heart of central Kentucky. Within this region a person can see agriculture hard at work. As technology has now become a common word with farming, there are still numerous tokens of our past. One of the most notable attributes is the barns of our region.

A barn is symbolic of the hours of hard work that every farmer has endured inside its walls. Within the floor one could find the sweat, blood, and tears that built the barn and kept it standing. The barns in this area are not only sturdy in their design, they have within them many stories of those early mornings, late nights, hot summers, and freezing winters. Regardless of their purpose—whether it is housing tobacco, hauling in hay, or watching the miracle of birth—each structure helps keep the lifeline of agriculture running strong.

Within these barns FFA members have developed their Agriculture Experience Projects and set the foundations for their futures. For some members, they started with just a few cows or a small part of their father's tobacco crop. Today those humble beginnings have evolved into complex farming operations that sustain life for these past members. FFA members have realized their dreams in these barns. For some it was to take the family farm, or to receive the coveted American FFA degree, or just to continue the love for agriculture. No matter what the dream, the barn has been there to cultivate the aspiration and to make it grow.

Anyone who has ever worked on a farm understands the importance of a barn. Its strong foundation has stood the test of time. These barns are as unique as the people who helped to construct them.

the FFA creed

"I believe in the future of agriculture, with a faith born not of words but of deeds—achievements won by the present and past generations of agriculturists; in the promise of better days through better ways, even as the better things we now enjoy have come to us from the struggles of former years.

"I believe that to live and work on a good farm, or to be engaged in other agricultural pursuits, is pleasant as well as challenging; for I know the joys and discomforts of agricultural life and hold an inborn fondness for those associations which, even in hours of discouragement, I cannot deny.

"I believe in leadership from ourselves and respect from others. I believe in my own ability to work efficiently and think clearly, with such knowledge and skill as I can secure, and in the ability of progressive agriculturists to serve our own and the public interest in producing and marketing the product of our toil.

"I believe in less dependence on begging and more power in bargaining; in the life abundant and enough honest wealth to help make it so—for others as well as myself; in less need for charity and more of it when needed; in being happy myself and playing square with those whose happiness depends upon me.

"I believe that American agriculture can and will hold true to the best traditions of our national life and that I can exert an influence in my home and community which will stand solid for my part in that inspiring task."

The creed was written by E. M. Tiffany and adopted at the Third National Convention of the FFA. It was revised at the thirty-eighth and the sixty-third conventions.

2000–2001 FFA officers

Kentucky FFA President—Julie P'Pool, Pennyrile Region

Kentucky FFA Vice President—Chad Aull, Green River Region

Kentucky FFA Secretary—Brandon Sowder, Northern Kentucky Region

Kentucky FFA Treasurer—Amanda Applegate, Licking River Region

Kentucky FFA Reporter—Marc Adams, Kentucky River Region

Kentucky FFA Sentinel—Brandon Davis, Lake Cumberland Region

Kentucky FFA Purchase Region Vice President—Ronza Childress

Kentucky FFA Barren River Region Vice President—Brent Fields

Kentucky FFA Lincoln Trail Region Vice President—Curtis Jones

Kentucky FFA Bluegrass River Region Vice President—Josh Long

FFA motto

Learning to Do,
Doing to Learn,
Earning to Live,
Living to Serve.

FFA emblem and colors

The FFA colors are designated as national blue and corn gold.

The cross section of the ear of corn provides the foundation of the emblem, just as corn has historically served as the foundation crop of American agriculture. It is also a symbol of unity, as corn is grown in every state of the nation.

The rising sun signifies progress and holds a promise that tomorrow will bring a new day glowing with opportunity.

The plow signifies labor and tillage of the soil, the backbone of agriculture and the historic foundation of our country's strength.

The eagle is a national symbol that serves as a reminder of our freedom and ability to explore new horizons for the future of agriculture.

The owl, long recognized for its wisdom, symbolizes the knowledge required to be successful in the industry of agriculture.

The words "Agricultural Education" and "FFA" are emblazoned in the center to signify the combination of learning and leadership necessary for progressive agriculture.

BLUEGRASS REGION

Hunterton Farm, North Middletown Road, Bourbon County, Kentucky. Fourteen-sided polygonal barn has a low roof with a single dormer and feed bins arranged continuously on the inside walls. Constructed around 1913. (Submitted by Rusty Speakes)

Runnymede Farm, Cynthiana Road, Bourbon County, Kentucky. Two-story stone barn, originally Cooper's Run Baptist Meeting House, circa 1800, also early meeting place for Bourbon County Court, later a hemp factory. Utilized as a horse barn since 1900. (Submitted by Rusty Speakes)

Hillside Farm, North Middletown Road, Bourbon
County, Kentucky. Early nineteenth-century
unchinked 10' x 13' x 8' log corncrib. Wood post
foundation with asphalt-shingle roof. Small grain chute
left of the front door. (Submitted by Rusty Speakes)

Xalapa Farm, Stoney Point Road, Bourbon County, Kentucky. Large thirty-four-stall stone-training barn built in the 1920s with monitored red-tile roof and curved ends. An indoor race track surrounds the stalls. (Submitted by Rusty Speakes)

Evergreen Farm, Escondida Road, Bourbon County, Kentucky. Quarried stone-foaling barn with clipped-end gables, hipped-roof dormers, and bracketed eaves. Original carriage elevator to move carriages to second-story loft is still operable. (Submitted by Rusty Speakes)

Stonerside Farm, North Middletown Road, Bourbon County, Kentucky. Horse barn displaying excellent cross-ventilation. (Submitted by Rusty Speakes)

Runnymede Farm, Cynthiana Road, Bourbon County, Kentucky. Narrow brick barn, originally a hemp factory, with shed roof, sandstone lintels and sills, and Flemish bond brickwork. Probably built just after the Civil War. (Submitted by Rusty Speakes)

English Farm, LaRue Road, Bourbon County,
Kentucky. One-hundred-year-old two-story
brick horse barn with jerkinheaded or clipped-
end gables and cupola ventilators. Probably built
by prominent Bourbon County businessman
G. W. Bowen. (Submitted by Rusty Speakes)

In the 1930s, R. H. Waller erected a five-story barn that he conceived as a prototype for taking the barn to the tobacco. This building is located between Old U.S. 62 and Old Oxford Pike, one-and-a-half miles northeast of Georgetown. There were catwalks inside the barn (p. 146) for workers to enter the rails to hang the sticks of tobacco; there was also a system of pulleys in place to raise the wagonload of tobacco into the barn to reduce the number of men required to hang the tobacco. To unload a wagon from the ground, seven men were required in the rails. This barn was designed to house thirty-two acres of tobacco as it was grown in the 1930s. (Submitted by Bill Mott)

This square barn with an octagonal cupola is a unique design for a tobacco and livestock barn in central Kentucky. The barn, nestled in a valley next to Little Eagle Creek, was built sometime during the late 1800s to early 1900s on the Edward Burgess Homestead. (Submitted by Bill Mott)

Big Barn

In 1893, this portion of the Horse Park was purchased by Mr. John D. Creighton and named Ashland-Wilkes Farm. Creighton was the first to breed and train Standardbreds on the land. In 1897, he constructed both the Park's 1/2 mile training track and the "Big Barn." In 1909, the farm was purchased by Lamon V. Harkness and became part of Walnut Hall Farm. Walnut Hall added on to the Big Barn and built the indoor auction area in the early 1900's. Walnut Hall Farm became the first major Kentucky Standardbred nursery to auction its yearlings on the premises.

The "Big Barn" has fifty-two 13' x 16' stalls, is 476 feet long and 75 feet wide. It remains one of the largest wooden horse barns in the world.

This barn was constructed in 1897 as part of a Standardbred Horse operation owned by John Creighton. The farm was purchased in the early 1900s by the Walnut Hall Farm, which became the Kentucky Horse Park in the 1970s. This is one of the largest wooden horse barns in the world; it measures 476 feet long by 75 feet wide and contains fifty-two 13' x 16' stalls. (Submitted by Bill Mott)

Newton Craig—nephew of Elijah Craig, Georgetown's founder—served as keeper of Kentucky's penitentiary from 1843 to 1855, utilizing this three-story rock and brick structure as a winery. Prisoners' labor was used to manufacture wine, whiskey, tombstones, furniture, picture frames, flour, and whiskey barrels, of which the keeper was to get one-third of the profits after $5,000. The structure has an elevator operated by a hand pulley system to increase efficiency. Source: *A History of Scott County, As Told by Selected Buildings* by Ann Bevins, 1981. (Submitted by Bill Mott)

The Floral Hall was erected in the 1880s on the site of land purchased by the Maxwell Springs Fair Association; the monies came from Congress as compensation for damages done by Union Troops. The first floor of the hall was devoted to horticultural and agricultural products; the second story was occupied with needlework, stitching, fancy work, etc.; the third floor, added in 1883 by the Fair of the A & M Association, was devoted to art. Seats were arranged in the center of the dome for fair visitors to look out on the gardens, fountains, bands, machinery, and livestock exhibits and trotting matches. The Floral Hall still stands on the grounds of the Red Mile Trotting Race Track, where fairs were held until the 1980s. (Submitted by Bill Mott)

The James Stone Whisky Warehouse is often the subject of speculation of travelers on Interstate 64 in western Scott County. This three-story ornate brick structure was built a short time after the 1850s and was used by Mr. Stone to produce and store an annual production of over 8,000 gallons. The distillery operated until the 1870s when it closed due to high taxes and a recession. The building is presently used for hay storage by the Greathouse family for their horse operation. Source: *A History of Scott County, As Told by Selected Buildings* by Ann Bevins, 1981. (Submitted by Bill Mott)

Every turn-of-the-century estate required a set of outbuildings that could support the horse-driven society of 1900. When John W. Osborne built his second home in Scott County in 1900, he erected this carriage barn in the board-and-batten Gothic influence. All prominent landowners of the nineteenth century built a mansion and all of the necessary outbuildings to impress others in their circle. The building photographed is located one-half mile north of Georgetown on the west side of the highway on U.S. 25. (Submitted by Bill Mott)

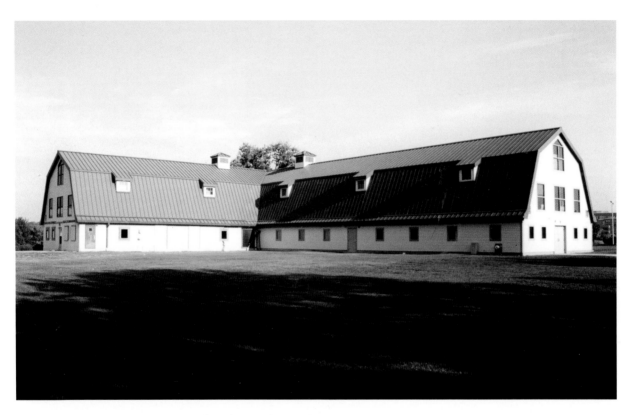

The E. S. Goodbarn was originally a dairy parlor on the University of Kentucky campus. The original portion of the research farm where the Goodbarn is located was purchased by the university in 1887 with money from the Hatch Act. It has been remodeled to look like the building that stands on the campus today, and it is now used for meetings and many other on-campus events. (Submitted by the Agricultural Education Society, University of Kentucky)

This beef show barn was located on the Coldstream Research Farm on the University of Kentucky campus in Lexington. It was originally used as a horse barn but was remodeled to be used as a beef show barn when the university took control of it in 1958. The barn was torn down and replaced by a research facility in the 1980s. (Submitted by the Agricultural Education Society, University of Kentucky)

This mule barn is over two hundred years old. Note the hand-hewn logs exposed at the end. The stone work was redone in the mid-1990s. This barn is located on the farm of the late John Thompson on Tyrone Pike in Versailles, Kentucky.

Scenic view of a thoroughbred horse barn
from the Versailles Bypass. Brookside Farm
is a complete thoroughbred operation.

This modern-styled tobacco barn was built in 1990. It has eight bents and four tiers. It also has an attached stripping room.

This barn is located four miles out on Ecton Road in rural Clark County and is owned by Geneva Wiseman. The original construction was only four bents; in the 1920s and in 1963, the back four bents were added on. The barn will hold up to 370 rails of tobacco. To the best of anyone's knowledge, the barn has had tobacco hung in it every year of its existence.

A small barn on Pig Branch
Road in Franklin County.
(Photo by Kim Brinegar)

This barn, located at 660 Crab Orchard
Road in Franklin County, is owned by Ray
Richardson. (Photo by Kim Brinegar)

Paschal True, now deceased, was a skilled building contractor who built 200 to 300 barns
throughout much of central Kentucky during his
lifetime. Until his retirement in 1984, he built
tobacco barns and feed and horse barns, and he
converted tobacco barns to horse barns when
the horse industry began to grow. (Submitted
by Ella True, Paschal True's wife; photos taken
by their granddaughter, Susan Shields)

Paschal True's feed barn in Stamping Ground, 1943

Dr. Ben Roach's Parrish
Hill Farm in Midway, 1965

J. T. Lundy's horse barn
in Scott County, 1980

SOURCES

There are many other resources for more information about FFA, Kentucky, agriculture, and barns available on the Internet. Some of the ones viewed during the creation of this book are listed here.

National FFA Organization
http://www.ffa.org

Kentucky's FFA Organization
http://www.kyffa.org

Kentucky's Official Web Site
http://www.kydirect.net/

Kentucky Tourism
http://www.kytourism.com

Education America
http://www.educationamerica.net/facts/ky_sfacts.html

Things To Do
http://www.thingstodo.com/states/ky/facts.htm

Why Are Barns Red?
http://museum.cl.msu.edu/barn/stories/story006/

Beacon Journal Article on Mail Pouch Ads
http://www.ohio.com/bj/fun/trav/mailpouch.html

Electronic Field Trip
http://frost.ca.uky.edu/pigtrip/crop2.htm

Bluegrass Agriculture
http://www.princeton.edu/~betsys/Agriculture.html

Kentucky Fast Facts and Trivia
http://www.50states.com/facts/kentucky.htm

Types of Barns
http://www.humanities.org/barnagain/variety.html

National Park Service Brief on Historic Barns
http://www2.cr.nps.gov/tps/briefs/brief20.htm

Kentucky Department of Agriculture
http://www.kyagr.com